NUTTY NATURE FACTS AND JOKES

I'm nutty about nature!

First published 2017 by Nosy Crow Ltd
The Crow's Nest, 10a Lant Street
London SE1 1QR

www.nosycrow.com

ISBN 978 0 85763 925 7

Text © Andy Seed 2017
Illustrations © Sarah Horne 2017

A CIP catalogue record for this book is available from the British Library.

Printed and bound in the UK by Clays Ltd, St Ives Plc.

Papers used by Nosy Crow are made from wood grown in
sustainable forests.

1 3 5 7 9 8 6 4 2

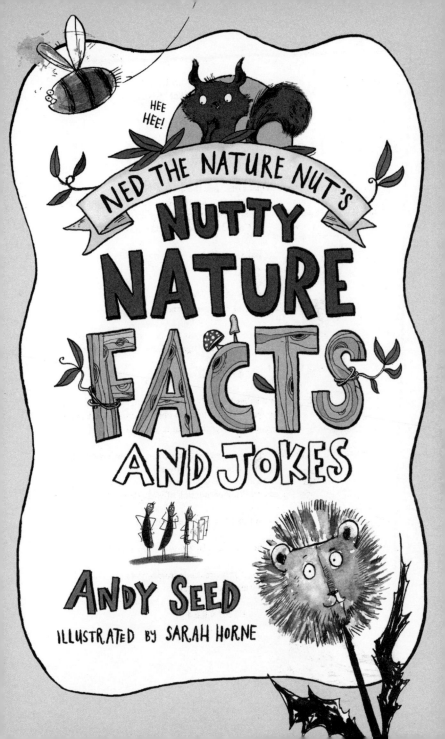

HEE HEE!

NED THE NATURE NUT'S
NUTTY
NATURE
FACTS
AND JOKES

ANDY SEED

ILLUSTRATED BY SARAH HORNE

Do you want to hear about the
hedgehog that went to the barber's?
There's no point.

What's the best animal to be
when you're cold?
A little otter.

MOUTHY MOTH FACT

The clothes moth does not eat at all (probably because it doesn't have a mouth!), but beware – its caterpillars eat woolly jumpers, socks and even carpets.

MUNCH
MUNCH
MUNCH
MUNCH

What has 100 legs but no sense?
A sillipede.

What's a butterfly's best
school subject?
Moths.

Where at school can you always
find an eagle?
In the dictionary.

Why are ladybirds no good at hide and seek?

They're always spotted.

What do you call a deer with no eyes?
No idea.

Where do spiders do most of their shopping?
On the web.

FIGHTY FACT

Male smooth snakes are not so smooth when it comes to competing for a female mate. They will grab and bite each other until one gives up and slinks off.

How do you keep flies out of the kitchen?

Put a bucket of poo in the living room.

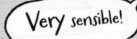

Very sensible!

THISTLY THACT

In Roman times, it was thought that eating thistles could cure **baldness**.

Why does nothing bother a quiet owl?

It doesn't give a hoot.

What is a toad's favourite film?
Star Warts.

How do herb gardens get so much done?
They have plenty of thyme.

What's a mouse's favourite game?
Hide and squeak.

SEASHORE STRANGENESS

These are all real animals found along the British coast:

Sea hare

Candy-striped flatworm

Rainbow leaf beetle

Bloody Henry

Sea gooseberry

Cornish sucker

Sea squirt

Purse sponge

These shore are silly!

12

Why is the seashore so strong?
It's got loads of mussels.

Did you hear about the ant who
fell over sixty feet?
He was trying to squeeze
past a centipede.

What's the best way to avoid
itches from biting gnats?

Don't bite any.

What is an octopus's favourite book?

Diary of a Wimpy Squid.

FLYING FACT

Flying squirrels can't actually fly, but they can glide from tree to tree using their own built-in parachute.

Just found out — I'm **not** a flying squirrel!

What's a rat's favourite country?

Gnaway.

WHICH BIRD...

Comes after 'i'?
A jay.

Collects stamps?
A hobby.

Can fill up your car?
A petrel.

Cheep laughs...

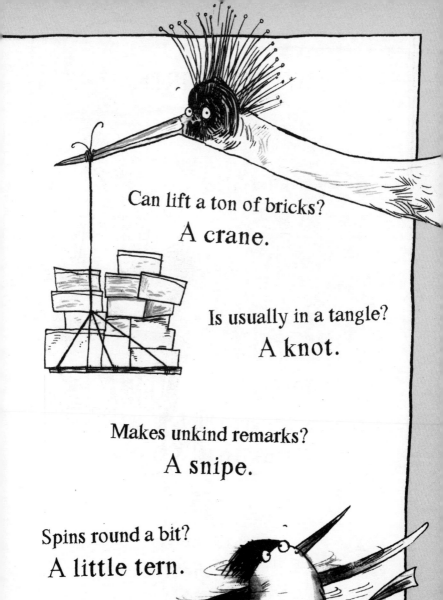

Can lift a ton of bricks?
A crane.

Is usually in a tangle?
A knot.

Makes unkind remarks?
A snipe.

Spins round a bit?
A little tern.

17

How do you fix a broken mushroom?
Using toad's tools.

What lives in the forest and
keeps birds dry?
A robin hood.

SNACKY FACT

The normal diet of the rare
pine marten is small animals
(especially grey squirrels) which
it chases through tree tops
at astonishing speed. However,
naturalists have also discovered
that this speedy hunter is wild
about peanut butter.

Peanut butter's
much nicer than
squirrel spread.

PEANUT
BUTTER

What happens when birds
drop out of the sky?

They use a sparrowchute.

IVY FACT

Ivy is a climbing plant that is poisonous to people but gives nectar and shelter to lots of animals, especially butterflies.

SALTY FACT

Seaweed is sometimes used as an ingredient of ice cream.

Yuk!

Why do geese fly south in winter?
It's too far to walk.

Did you hear about the ladybird
who punched a fox?
**It was the beetles'
greatest hit.**

What has a head like a deer,
a body like a deer and feet like
a deer but isn't a deer?
A fawn.

Why are fish never goalkeepers?
They're afraid of
the nets.

OINKY BADGER FACT

The Welsh word for badger is 'mochyn daear', which means 'earth pig'.

Where do rabbits buy their clothes?

From the hare dresser.

FROGGY FACT

Frogs don't drink water through their mouths but absorb it through their skin. They can also breathe through their skin when hibernating. Some species of frog shed their skin, like a snake... and then eat it!

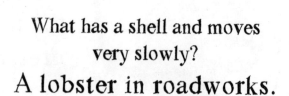

What has a shell and moves very slowly?

A lobster in **roadworks.**

SUE: How do you tell the difference between sheep poo and chocolate raisins?

HUGH: I don't know.

SUE: In that case, I'll buy the sweets.

I prefer choccy peanuts. Well, to sheep poo anyway!

What did one fern say
to the other?
Will you be my frond?

What's at the end of a rainbow?
A 'w'.

What holds up a squirrel's roof?
Walnuts.

PRICKLY FACT

Blackberries are sometimes used by forensic botanists* to solve crimes. This is because brambles often grow where a body has been buried in secret after a murder.

*Plant scientists who are also detectives. Cool job!

OSPREY FACT

Ospreys fly from the UK to Africa
(about 3,000 miles) when they are
just twelve weeks old. At that age a
human baby can't even sit up!

Why can't you buy
a pair of stags?

They're two deer.

Doe!

HARD THINGS TO SPOT
IN THE COUNTRYSIDE

A badger with a badge.

A fox wearing
foxgloves.

A rabbit saying ribbit.

A bluebell that rings.

WHICH BIRD...

Steals a lot?
A robin.

Holds up flowers?
A stork.

Is always gulping?
A swallow.

Flies with a string?
A kite.

Is always wet?
A dipper.

Is always out of breath?
A puffin.

Why did the ant get wet?
Because the centipede.

How do you know carrots are
good for your eyes?
Have you ever seen a
rabbit wearing glasses?!

STINKY FACT

Hedgehog poo looks like slugs.

Rabbit poo looks like raisins.

Mouse poo looks like black rice.

Spider poo looks like
salt and pepper.

Mine smells
of roses... not!

BATTY FACT

The pipistrelle bat weighs less
than a two pence piece.

They're light
and cheap!

Why don't owls go courting in the rain?
It's too wet to woo.

Did you hear about the frog
with the broken leg?

He was very unhoppy.

Why did the crab wear a jumper?

It was feeling a
bit nippy.

What's thin and green and
has 10,000 eyes?

Grass.
I lied about the eyes.

What do giant space squirrels eat?
Astronuts.

FARTY FACT

The cockroach is the fartiest creature in the UK. The scuttling insect releases more smelly gas for its size than any other animal.

I've done a **phew** myself...

NAUGHTY FACT

Wood ants live in giant nests of up to 100,000 insects. Each ant can lift over 100 times its own body weight. But be careful if you go near their nests because they can squirt acid at you!

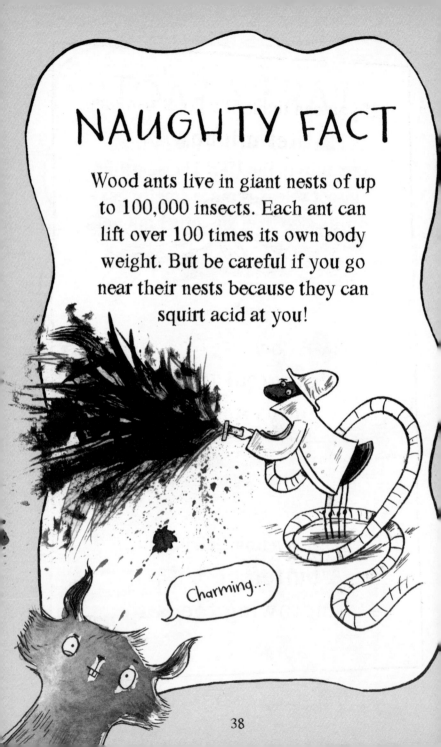

Charming...

If you can think of a good fish pun,
let minnow.

Why do kids love the seaside?
It's a great place for
buoys and gulls.

What's yellow and hobbles?
A buttercup with an
ingrowing toenail.

FEARSOME FACT

These wild animals are no longer
found in Britain:

BEAST	
Wolf	. . . .
Bear	. . . .
Wolverine	. . . .
Mammoth	. . . .
Sabre-toothed tiger	. . . . . .
Dinosaur	. . . .

LAST SEEN

. . . .	350 years ago
. . . .	1,300 years ago
. . . .	8,000 years ago
. . . .	14,000 years ago
. . . .	28,000 years ago
. . . .	65,000,000 years ago

BUZZY FACT

A bumblebee flaps its wings over 120 times every second.

Bumblebees never stop at traffic lights… because they can't see the colour red.

TITCHY FACT

Duckweeds are the smallest plants you can find. They grow on ponds and each one is a tiny leaf-like green blob only 3–4 mm long.

Why didn't the prawn and the lobster share their sweets?

They're two shellfish.

THINGS TO AVOID ON A COUNTRY RAMBLE

1. **Ants** in your pants

2. **Shrews** in your shoes

3. **A goat** in your coat

4. **Cress** in your dress

A **snail** in your tail's quite annoying too!

44

5. Doves in your gloves

6. Mites in your tights

7. A fox in your socks

8. Fruit in your suit

EGGY FACT

Eels are very long, thin fish covered in a layer of protective slime. They can live for up to 50 years. How and where eels lay eggs has never been observed. It's thought to happen in a place called the Sargasso Sea, thousands of miles from the UK, but it remains a mystery of nature.

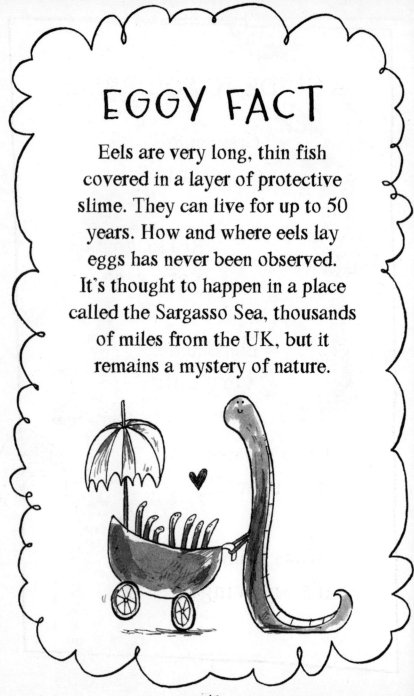

A GUIDE TO SQUIRRELS

Grey squirrel:
very common

Red squirrel:
very rare

Blue squirrel:
very cold

Green squirrel:
very unwell

White squirrel:
it's snowing!

What's a hedgehog's
favourite food?

Prickled onions.

What happens when a
frog breaks down?

It gets toad away.

How many tickles does it take to
make an octopus laugh?

Ten tickles.

JUMPY FACT

Salmon travel up rivers to lay their eggs and they will leap up to three metres out of the water to clear waterfalls and weirs.

I get my eggs from the supermarket...

What does it cost to send a cuttlefish to the vet?
Six quid.

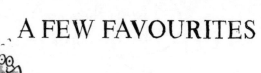

A FEW FAVOURITES

BEE

Favourite toy:
Buzzzz Lightyear

Favourite clothes:
Leg swarmers

Favourite haircare product:
Honeycomb

Favourite holiday destination:
Hastings

Favourite film:
Stung Fu Panda

Favourite car:
A Hummer

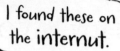

I found these on the internut.

TREE

Favourite toy:
Bud Lightyear

Favourite clothes:
Fir coat

Favourite haircare product:
Pear dryer

Favourite holiday destination:
The beech

Favourite film:
Bark to the Future

Favourite car:
Aspen Martin

BITEY FACT

Moles create special underground larders where they store worms to eat (after first biting off their heads). Sometimes there are over 100 live worms in these chambers.

Have you ever seen a fin whale?
No, but I've seen
a fat one.

FURRY FACT

A squirrel's tail comes in useful as a handy umbrella. Squirrels use them to keep rain and snow off when the weather is grotty.

HUNGRY FACT

The butterwort is a harmless-looking plant but one that is deadly to insects. Small flies land on its sticky leaves which then curl around the insects so the plant can eat them.

You'd **butter** believe it!

KNOW YOUR BIRDS

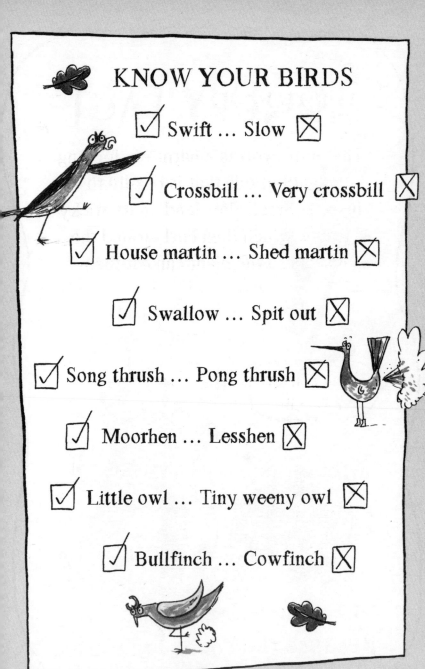

☑ Swift ... Slow ☒

☑ Crossbill ... Very crossbill ☒

☑ House martin ... Shed martin ☒

☑ Swallow ... Spit out ☒

☑ Song thrush ... Pong thrush ☒

☑ Moorhen ... Lesshen ☒

☑ Little owl ... Tiny weeny owl ☒

☑ Bullfinch ... Cowfinch ☒

TOOTHY FACT

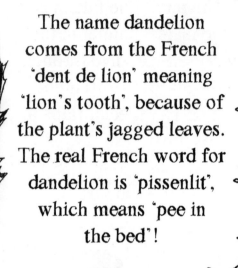

The name dandelion comes from the French 'dent de lion' meaning 'lion's tooth', because of the plant's jagged leaves. The real French word for dandelion is 'pissenlit', which means 'pee in the bed'!

What is a hedgehog's favourite fruit?
A spineapple.

Why do owls hunt for food at night?
Because the shops are closed.

FAST FACT

The peregrine falcon is the fastest animal in the world. It can dive through the air up to 240 mph! And it has special flaps in its nostrils so the air doesn't go up its nose too fast.

VAROOM

How do squirrels keep their nests free from dirt?

They go to the drey cleaners.

A drey is a squirrel's nest. No, I didn't know that either!

DEADLY FACT

Britain has several poisonous
wild plants including these
dangerous beauties:

Hemlock

Wolfsbane

Cuckoo pint

Deadly nightshade

What's a bee's favourite city?
Stingapore.

Where do you find bees in a queue?
At the buzz stop.

What's a crab's favourite
card game?

Snap.

Which fish is the best climber?

A mountain pike.

What has eight legs and takes
kids to school?

An octobus.

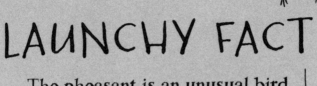

LAUNCHY FACT

The pheasant is an unusual bird because it takes off almost vertically when flying.

I can take off vertically: **downwards!**

What's a rabbit's favourite film?
Bunny I Shrunk the Kids.

STINGY FACT

The beadlet anemone, found in rock pools, looks like a blob of red jelly but it has 192 stinging tentacles used to catch and stun passing prey.

What's the difference between a fly and a bird?

A bird can fly but a fly can't bird.

And a squirrel can't DJ!

FUNGI FACT

The giant puffball is a type of mushroom that can grow as large as a basketball. A puffball can produce seven trillion spores – that's 7,000,000,000,000!

PAINFUL FACT

Stinging nettle leaves have tiny glass-like hairs containing formic acid. When we touch a leaf the hairs inject us with toxins causing a 'sting'. Nettle fibres can be woven into fabric to make clothes – the German army made uniforms from them in World War I.

What happened to the boy who
tried to catch fog?

He mist.

Even I wouldn't
try that...

What do clouds put on
after a shower?

Thunderwear.

KNOW YOUR NATURE

A jellyfish is not a fish.

A polecat is not a cat.

A slow worm is not a worm.

A dandelion is not a lion.

A **toadstool** is not a piece of furniture.

A **nightjar** is not a glass container.

A **foxglove** is not something to wear on your hands.

A **magpie** is not a pastry dish.

What is winter's
favourite saying?

There's no business like
snow business!

Why are bird spotters often on
the ground?

Because they're always
shouting 'Duck!'.

HEAVY FACT

An average male grey seal weighs about 230kg – that's the same as 700 red squirrels!

Erk, I hope they don't live in **trees!**

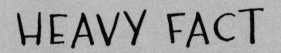

FIGHTY FACT

Some types of dragonfly fight each other in mid-air to defend their territories over ponds.

FAMOUS PEOPLE WHO LOVE NATURE

William Snakespeare

Queen Victoria Plum

Wayne Pruney

Ladybird Gaga

Prawn French

Elvis Parsley

Justin Beaver

What are caterpillars scared of?
Dogerpillars.

How do blackbirds get into
your house?
Through the jackdaw.

Cheeky beaky!

How do you hire a squirrel?
Put it up a ladder.

HARD FACT

The piddock is a shellfish creature
that can drill holes in rocks.

What's a rabbit's favourite book?
Warren Peace.

WEIRD WILD FLOWERS

Some of Britain's wild flowers have very odd names:

Bogbean

Cowslip

Whoops!

Creeping Jenny

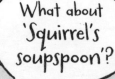

What about 'Squirrel's soupspoon'?

Fat hen

Lady's bedstraw

Mouse-ear

Petty spurge

Pignut

75

ANIMALS' FAVOURITE FILMS

Dog
The Hound of Music

Cat
Mice Age

Dinosaur
Bite at the Museum

All made in Hollywoodn't!

Bee
The Lion Sting

Bear
Hairy Poppins

Flea
The Lion, the Itch and the Wardrobe

Wasp
Despicable Bee

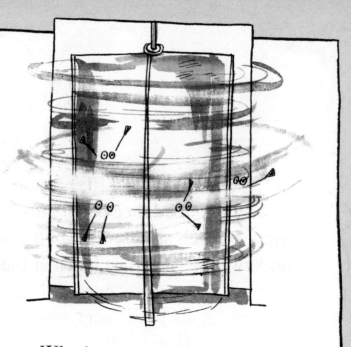

What's green and goes round
and round?

A frog stuck in a revolving
door.

Why didn't the blackthorn
fruit get the joke?

It was a little sloe.

BRIEF FACT

Mayflies are insects with a strange life cycle. They start life as eggs on a river bed then hatch into nymphs which usually live for a year underwater. They then hatch at the surface becoming winged insects. Sadly, some of the adults only live for a day.

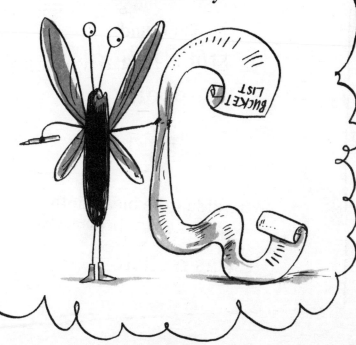

FUNNY FUNGI

There are lots of mushrooms and toadstools with wacky names:

Candle snuff fungus

Chicken of the woods

Destroying angel

Stinkhorn

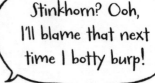

Stinkhorn? Ooh, I'll blame that next time I botty burp!

Hare's ear

Shaggy ink cap

Scarlet elf cup

Turkey tail

Wood blewit

Parrot wax cap

What do squirrels do at
the top of trees?
Highbernate.

What do squirrels give each other
on Valentine's Day?
Forget-me-nuts.

What do you call a cat with
eight legs?
An octopuss.

WEEDY FACT

Beware of giant hogweed! This monster wild flower can grow four metres (over 12 feet) high, and has sap which can cause nasty skin burns. It is against the law to plant giant hogweed in the UK.

What clucks and clicks?
A ballpoint hen.

PECKY FACT

Woodpeckers sometimes drum on metal parts of telegraph poles to make a loud rattle and let others know their territory.

Why don't they use one of these?

Why did the whale cross the sea?
To get to the other tide.

How do seagulls communicate
over long distances?

They use squawky-talkies.

What's big, green, has a trunk
and leaves?

A sick elephant at a party.

BIRDS' TOP TV SHOWS

Eagle
Match of the Prey

Budgie
Coronation Tweet

Owl
Doctor Woo

Chicken
The Eggs Factor

Duck
The Great British
Drake Off

LEGGY FACT 1

Millipedes have between
36 and 400 legs.

LEGGY FACT 2

If a shore crab loses a leg,
it simply grows a new one.

I wish that
happened each time
I lost a hazelnut...

GREEDY FACT

Some bats can eat 3,000 insects in one night.

Huh, I could eat 3,000 nuts in an hour — if I could just remember where I buried them...

How do squirrels get on social media?
Using the internut.

What's pink and does
85 miles per hour?

A worm in a bobsleigh.

What's a deer's favourite food?

Doe nuts.

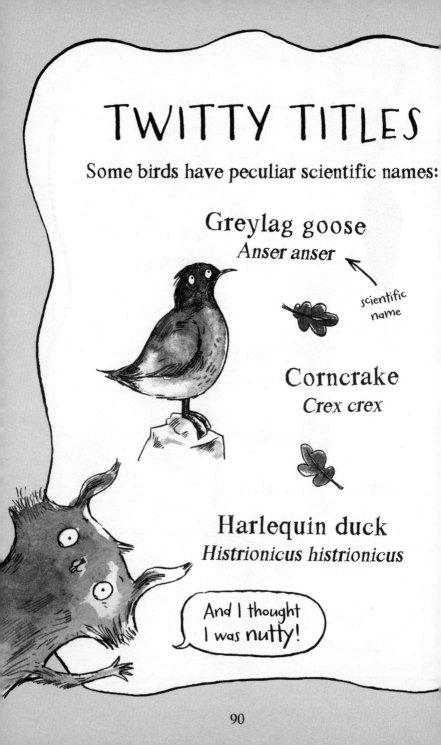

TWITTY TITLES

Some birds have peculiar scientific names:

Greylag goose
Anser anser

scientific name

Corncrake
Crex crex

Harlequin duck
Histrionicus histrionicus

And I thought I was **nutty**!

Scops Owl
Otus scops

Swift
Apus apus

Wren
Troglodytes troglodytes

Desert warbler
Sylvia nana

Hobby
Falco subbuteo

FLIGHTY FACT

Swifts are fast-flying birds that spend amazing amounts of time in the air. Except when nesting, swifts fly continuously, sometimes not landing for ten months at a time! They eat insects caught in flight and can drink, mate and sleep while flying.

 Which owl lives in the kitchen?
A teatowel.

What time do ducks get up
in the morning?
At the quack of dawn.

Why do herons have
long necks?
Because their
feet smell.

What's a teacher's
favourite minibeast?
A tick.

NESTY FACT

Birds have been known make their nests in unusual places, such as these:

In pockets of **jeans** on a washing line

On top of **traffic lights**

In the mouth of a giant **replica T-Rex**

In postboxes

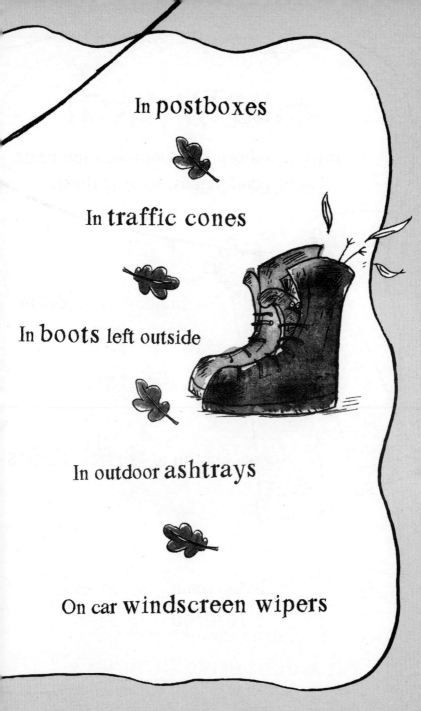

In traffic cones

In boots left outside

In outdoor ashtrays

On car windscreen wipers

BENDY FACT

Hazel trees are incredibly bendy – you can even tie thin branches in a knot!

Why don't squirrels own cars?
It would drive them nuts.

What's purple and as tall as a bus?
A plum on stilts.

Which insect is the quietest?
A mumble bee.

What's the first thing a shark eats
after having a tooth removed?
The dentist.

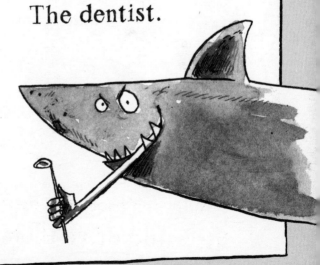

FISHY FACTS

Here are some facts about the UK's scariest freshwater fish: the pike.

The pike is a predator which specialises in ambushing other fish.

In some places pike are cannibals, with large pike feeding on smaller ones.

Right, I'm cancelling that swim in the pond...

In spring, a quarter of a female's body weight is made up of **eggs**.

Pike occasionally catch **ducklings** and other water birds.

The largest pike caught in Britain weighed over 21 kg and was well over **a metre** long.

ANIMALS' FAVOURITE SPORTS

Rodents – Mice skating

Fish – Skateboarding

Toads – Tug of Wart

Horse – Stable tennis

Squirrels – Nutball

Whale – Squash

Pig – Ice hoggy

ANIMALS' TOP TV SHOWS

Cow
Moo Peter

Stag
Top Deer

Pig
Fireman Ham

Sheep
Have I Got News for Ewe

Amphibian
Have I Got Newts for You

Harpy
Beastenders

Insect
Postman Gnat

Bee
Strictly Hum Dancing

NESTY FACT

Squirrels make their nests, or dreys, from leaves, straw, twigs and grass, but in towns they sometimes use litter such as crisp packets and drinking straws.

But don't try old supermarket trolleys – it's really hard getting them up a tree.

What do you call a girl with a frog on her head?

Lily.

RATTY FACT

Black rats can climb brick walls and walk across telephone wires.

FLUTTERY FACT

Snowflakes are actually clear, not white. Snow reflects light which makes it appear white.

What's brown and smells?
A squirrel's nose.

I couldn't do **whiffout** it.

How do you stop foxes
from pooing on the lawn?

Let them in the house.

Which creepy-crawly has antlers?

A deerwig.

Why are trees careless?

**They're always losing
their leaves.**

CATTY FACTS

Here are some true things about
Scottish wildcats:

Wildcats are extremely **rare**.

Wildcats **purr** but they do not miaow.

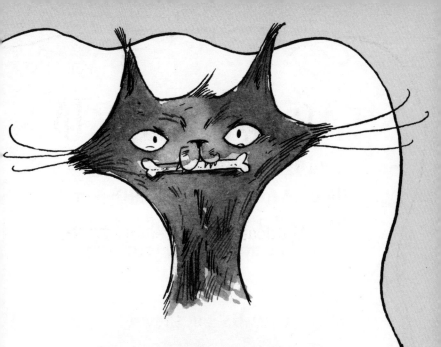

Their main **prey** is rabbits and
they eat nearly every part,
including the bones.

They avoid any **human contact**.

Wildcats' **hearing** is amazingly
sensitive, as is their **night vision**.

FAR BACK FACT

Britain's most ancient tree is thought to be a yew in Fortingall, Scotland. Experts estimate that it could be up to 3,000 years old.

Yew must be kidding!

ANIMALS' FAVOURITE SONGS

Frog
The Hokey Croaky

Bug
Silent Mite

Skunk
Jingle Smells

Fish
Amazing Dace

Dung Beetle
I Will Always Love Poo

Bird
Head, Shoulders, Knees & Crows

Sea mammals
The Whales on the Bus

THINGS YOU CAN'T DO IN THE COUNTRYSIDE

1. Ring a **bluebell**

2. Have a drink of tea in a **buttercup**

I tried to lock a door with a donkey.

3. Stub a **mistletoe**

4. Spend the night in a **mushroom**

5. Tie a **rainbow**

6. Play cricket with a
long-eared bat

7. Wear an **earwig**

SWIMMY FACT

Cormorants are birds that are champion swimmers. They dive underwater in both the sea and rivers to chase and catch fish. Amazingly, their feathers are not even waterproof!

What do you call 85 squirrels
on a road?

A tailback.

And it's really hard
to bury acorns in
tarmac...

What happened when two
swans had a race?

They finished neck and neck.

Why don't weasels
use email?

They prefer
texting.

BEEP
BEEP!

SEAWEEDY FACTS

Lots of seaweeds have wacky names,
including these:

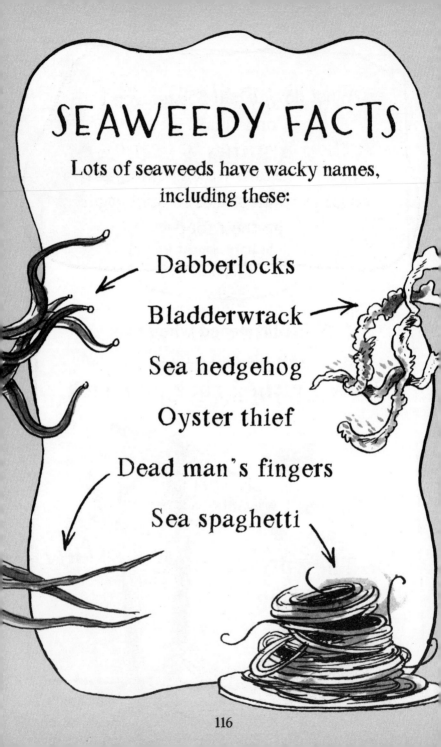

Dabberlocks

Bladderwrack

Sea hedgehog

Oyster thief

Dead man's fingers

Sea spaghetti

GRINDY FACT

Birds have a special stomach called a gizzard which sometimes contains small stones to help grind up their food.

Why did the owl 'owl?
Cos the woodpecker
would peck 'er.

A GUIDE TO WILD FLOWERS

Forget-me-not
Common plant with small blue flowers

Forget-me-knot
Boy scouts hate this plant

Forget-me-yacht
Usually grows in harbours

Forget-me-grot
Not the most beautiful bloom

Forget-me-snot
Claimed to cure a bad cold

Forget-me-spot
Teenagers like this a lot

MIGHTY FACT

The strongest natural material in the world is found in limpet teeth. These small shelled creatures cling to rocks and use their tiny teeth to scrape food off the surface. The second strongest natural material is spider silk.

How do flatfish get on social media?

Using Plaicebook.

Or Finstagram maybe?

HAIRY FACT

Many large moths develop from cute-looking hairy caterpillars. Beware of stroking these if you find one – sometimes their hairs can give you a nasty skin rash.

WHICH WILD FLOWER...

Causes accidents on farms?
A cowslip.

Soon melts?
A snowdrop.

Welcomes ships?
A dock.

Never says, "Who are you?"
Forget-me-not.

Is found under hens?
Chickweed.

Should you stay out of the way of?
A bullrush.

Where do you find giant termites?
**It depends where you
left them.**

Why is a crab apple small
and green?
**Because if it was large
and red it would be a
fire engine.**

SNAPPY FACT

If you look under flat stones in shallow, fast-flowing hill streams you might see a creature with large claws which looks like a mini-lobster. This is the freshwater crayfish – a rare animal that uses its powerful nippy claws to fight with.

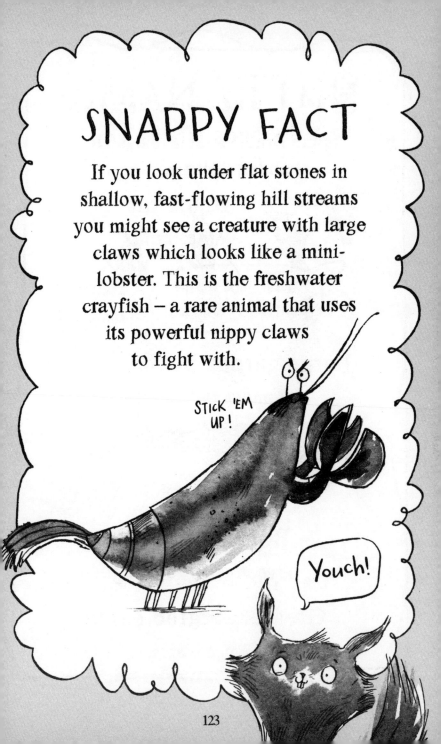

NUTTY NAMES

Some British animals have very strange scientific names:

Black rat
Rattus rattus

I think mine must be Nuttus maximus!

Badger
Meles meles

Large garden bumblebee
Bombus ruderatum

Grass snake
Natrix natrix

Bottlenose whale
Hyperoodon ampullatus

Greater spotted eagle
Clanga clanga

Why do forest woodpeckers
get their food from trees?

**Because supermarkets
won't deliver there.**

Have you ever seen a cricket bat?

**No, but I've seen
a dog bowl.**

What's got six legs and can fly?

Three sparrows.

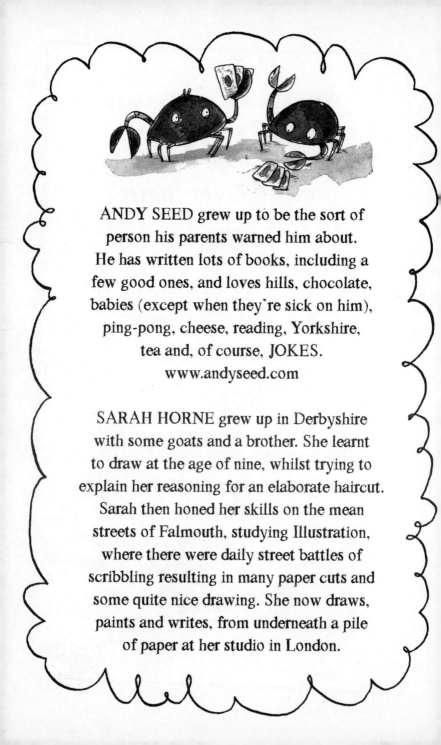

ANDY SEED grew up to be the sort of person his parents warned him about. He has written lots of books, including a few good ones, and loves hills, chocolate, babies (except when they're sick on him), ping-pong, cheese, reading, Yorkshire, tea and, of course, JOKES.
www.andyseed.com

SARAH HORNE grew up in Derbyshire with some goats and a brother. She learnt to draw at the age of nine, whilst trying to explain her reasoning for an elaborate haircut. Sarah then honed her skills on the mean streets of Falmouth, studying Illustration, where there were daily street battles of scribbling resulting in many paper cuts and some quite nice drawing. She now draws, paints and writes, from underneath a pile of paper at her studio in London.